Other "Little Books of Wisdom" Titles Available

T0040492

THE PHILLIES FAN'S LITTLE BOOK
OF WISDOM

THE PHILLIES FAN'S LITTLE BOOK
OF WISDOM

Sue Marquette Poremba

TAYLOR TRADE PUBLISHING
Lanham • Boulder • New York • Toronto • Plymouth, UK

Published by Taylor Trade Publishing
An imprint of The Rowman & Littlefield Publishing Group, Inc.
4501 Forbes Boulevard, Suite 200, Lanham, Maryland 20706

Distributed by NATIONAL BOOK NETWORK

Library of Congress Cataloging-in-Publication Data

Poremba, Sue Marquette.
 The Phillies fan's little book of wisdom / Sue Marquette Poremba.— 1st Taylor Trade Pub. ed.
   p. cm.
 ISBN 1-58979-307-2 (pbk. : alk. paper)
 1. Philadelphia Phillies (Baseball team)—Anecdotes. 2. Philadelphia Phillies (Baseball team)—Humor.
 I. Title.
 GV875.45P67 2006
 796.357'64097481—dc22   2005027897

∞™The paper used in this publication meets the minimum requirements of American National Standard for Information Sciences—Permanence of Paper for Printed Library Materials, ANSI/NISO Z39.48-1992.
Manufactured in the United States of America.

Dedication

To my family

• Acknowledgments •

A quick thanks to a couple of people who deserve a lot more than thanks: my parents, who made sure I got to a Phillies game at least once every summer; Jack, Jodi, Nola, Ann, Maureen, and Maggie, who have patiently listened to me chatter about the Phillies and writing; Gary, who gives me a reality check on everything I write; and most importantly, to the three people who put up with me daily. Jack, Kristy, and Dylan—I couldn't do this without your love, support, and encouragement.

• Introduction •

"I can't believe you like those bums."

That's what my dad's friends said to me in 1974 when I announced that I was a Phillies fan. I was eleven years old that summer, and the history of the team was still unknown to me. All I knew was that I discovered baseball, and the Phillies were the team that I chose.

But my dad and his friends knew that the Phillies had a sorry history. This was a team with the 1964 collapse, the 23-game losing streak of 1961, and only one win in the post-season. My parents and their friends were Yankees fans at that time—a bunch of winners, I was repeatedly reminded.

Still, my eleven-year-old self was stubborn, and I argued that the Phillies were a good team. Moreso, I decided, they were going to win because I watched them. One of the adults offered to bet me a quarter that the Phillies wouldn't finish above fourth place. I told him that I didn't want to take his money.

The Phillies finished in third place in 1974. By the end of the decade, the people who scoffed me had jumped on the Phillies bandwagon. And as far as I know, none of them has yet to jump off.

I came to the Phillies as they entered their golden age. In the first 10 years I followed the team, they contended for the division title, or at least had a respectable record. My Phillies had Mike Schmidt, Greg Luzinski, Garry Maddox, Manny Trillo, Bob Boone, Steve Carlton, Larry Christenson, Tug McGraw, and Larry Bowa. I literally grew up with these guys. They won their World Series days before my 18th birthday.

The team of my youth was dismantled during those years I was in college. A new team was put together, one that linked the old players of Schmidty and Lefty with new young players like Hayes and Franco with grizzled veterans from other teams, like Morgan and Perez and Denny. The 1983 team played in the World Series. I was a senior in college. This was not the team of my youth. I watched the Series, of course. Philadelphia was still my team, even with all of those former Reds players, but it wasn't quite the same.

The Phillies returned to their losing roots after 1983, and I moved out of Pennsylvania. But once the Phillies are in your blood, no other team can ever replace them. They were—they are—my team. By the time the 1993 team took baseball by surprise, I had turned my four-year-old boy into a life-long Phillies fan. He and I listened to every game on the radio. His favorite player was the guy who wore number 10 (Darren Daulton), like my all-time favorite player did twenty years earlier (Larry Bowa). This was the team of my contemporaries.

Baseball rules the summer in my family. We watch or listen to the guys on TV and radio who have a Phillies connection: John Kruk, Larry Bowa, Jeff Brantley, Tim McCarver, Larry Andersen, and Joe Morgan. I was a teenager during the successful run of the 1970s. My son is a teenager now, during what might be the second most successful run in Phillies history (in the terms of wins and losses). His heroes are Jimmy Rollins, Billy Wagner, Bobby Abreu, and Ryan Madsen. I'm hoping he gets to see them win a World Series soon.

Over the past thirty years, I've learned a lot more about Phillies history, and I understand now why, in 1974, people were so incredulous that this was my team. The Phillies have lost more games than any other team. They played in awful stadiums. Team owners traded away the star players in order to avoid paying them more money, and instead of putting a quality team on the field, the Phillies were more often than not a band of misfits (even the 1993 team fit that bill: "We're a throwback, all right," said John Kruk in response to the media reporting the team was a throwback to the old days. "Thrown back from other organizations."). Many players hated being there. Curt Flood fought against coming to Philadelphia and gave birth to free agency.

Yet, a team can't be in existence for over 120 years without having shining moments. We had the greatest third baseman of all time for his entire career. Arguably the best season ever by pitcher was had by Steve Carlton in 1972. The best offensive outfield of all time played for the Phillies. The team has had its share of Hall of Famers, Cy Young and Gold Glove winners, and Players of the Week. Bobby Abreu brought smiles to Philadelphia with his 2005 Home Run Derby power.

Phillies baseball is handed down from mother or father to son or daughter. It has connected me and my dad just like it has connected me and my son. It is a love affair that runs deeper than winning and losing. Being a Phillies fan is something that becomes a part of you for life.

You've Got to Start Somewhere

It took 33 seasons for the Phillies to win their first National League pennant. The Phils won the first game of the 1915 World Series, beating the Boston Red Sox by a score of 3-1. They didn't win a second World Series game until 1980.

Now, Which Team Is Yours?

For half a century, Philadelphia hosted two baseball teams: the Phillies and the Athletics. The Phillies first owner was Al Reach, owner of a local sporting goods company. The A's majority owner was Ben Shibe—Al Reach's business partner.

Put This One in the Win Column . . .

West Virginian Gene Kelly was hired as a Phillies radio announcer in 1950. Unlike By Saam, who stuck to the action on the field, Kelly added a lot of flair to his game calls. He came up with the term Fightin' Phils: "Tug on your caps, boys and girls, rub your noses, and let's get our Fightin' Phils some runs."

Understatement

When the Athletics entered the American League in 1901, the team signed away many players from the woeful Phillies. Manager Connie Mack wrote about this in his autobiography: "Our rivals, the Phillies, were not happy over our invasion of Philadelphia."

Don't Blink or You'll Miss It

Games pitched by Hall of Famer Grover Cleveland Alexander rarely
lasted more than 90 minutes.

Dream Outfield

In the 1890s, the Phillies put together what remains arguably the best offensive outfield in baseball history. Ed Delahanty, Big Sam Thompson, and Sliding Billy Hamilton are all in the Hall of Fame today. In 1892, the three outfielders batted over .300. In 1894, each one had a batting average over .400.

Are You a Cigar or a Ball Team?

In 1942, the Phillies temporarily changed their name to "Phils" because they couldn't financially afford a lawsuit with the Bayuk Cigar Company over the name.

Not to Be Confused with Toronto

In 1944, owner Bob Carpenter decided the team needed a new name. The team became known as the Blue Jays. A patch of a blue jay was attached to the left sleeve, but the name Phillies was never removed from the front of the jersey. No one paid much attention to the new name, and in a few years, the team re-established the Phillies name.

Red Team in a Blue City

When Philadelphia was a two-team city, it was generally accepted that Republicans followed the A's, while Democrats were Phillies fans. During the Athletics' run as a championship-caliber team, Republicans had a stronghold on the city's government. In 1950, the Phillies shocked the baseball world by going to the World Series, and the Democrats shocked the political world by taking over Philadelphia's City Hall. The A's moved to Kansas City a few years later, and the Republicans moved to the suburbs.

The Wrong Way

On July 4, 1976, in Pittsburgh, catcher Tim McCarver hit a home run with the bases loaded. The ball barely cleared the outfield fence, so Garry Maddox, the runner at first base, waited to make sure the ball would not be caught. McCarver jogged right past Maddox. Instead of a grand slam, McCarver was credited with a three-run single.

The Right Way

On July 4, 2005, in Pittsburgh, right fielder Bobby Abreu hit a home run with the bases loaded. He properly followed the baserunners and was credited with a grand slam home run.

Speaking of Grand Slams . . .

Three Phillies players slugged a grand slam for their first Major League hit. Utility player Jim Command did it in 1954. Second baseman Chase Utley hit his in 2003. Pitcher Bill "Frosty" Duggleby hit his in 1898 in his first major league at-bat.

As Long as They Aren't All Bad

"It's not a good place to have bad teams. On fan appreciation day, they slashed my tires."—Terry Francona, manager of the Phillies, 1997–2000.

Eventually, Someone Will Do It Perfectly

Jim Bunning's perfect game against the Mets on June 21, 1964, was the first one in the National League since 1880.

Not Perfect But Pretty Darn Good

On June 23, 1971, Rick Wise pitched a no-hitter. A walked batter prevented a perfect game. However, Wise made up for it by hitting two home runs in a 4-0 win over Cincinnati.

Home Field Advantage

Since their inception in 1883, the Phillies have
called 5 ball parks home:

Recreation Park, 1883–1886
Baker Bowl, 1887–1937
Shibe Park (later renamed Connie Mack Stadium), 1938–1970
Veteran's Stadium, 1971–2003
Citizens Bank Park, 2004–Present

Don't Give Starbucks Any Ideas

"Hitting him was like trying to drink coffee with a fork."—Pittsburgh Pirate first baseman Willie Stargell on batting against Steve Carlton.

Down on the Farm

Reading, Pa. became a minor league town in the 1880s. It became the home of the Phillies Double-A farm team in 1967, making it one of the longest major league/minor league associations in baseball.

Death to Flying Things

Bob Ferguson was a player-manager on the first Phillies team. He got the nickname "Death to Flying Things" because of his prowess as a second baseman. As a manager, Ferguson was a tyrant, which is why his managerial duties lasted only 17 days. However, he remained in charge of the team's financial matters throughout the year. Apparently, his real skill was with money because, even though the team was an utter failure on the field, the team actually finished the year in the black.

Before Bad Trades, There Was Typhoid Fever

Charley Ferguson was the Phillies' version of Babe Ruth. Ferguson played second base or center field on the days he wasn't pitching. Through his four years with the Phillies, he had 99 wins, including a no hitter, with a 2.67 ERA and a batting average of .288. He was touted as the future of the team after his breakthrough 1887 season. But right before spring training in 1888, Ferguson developed typhoid fever and died within three weeks at the age of 25.

Who Needs a Day Off?

Over a five-day period in 1908, late-season call-up Harry Coveleski pitched three games against John McGraw's New York Giants. Between September 29 and October 3, Coveleski beat the Giants 7-0, 6-2, and 3-2. These three losses forced the Giants into a playoff game with the Cubs, which the Giants lost. The Cubs, of course, went on to win the World Series.

Show Me the Money

On December 11, 1917, Phillies owner William Baker traded Grover Cleveland Alexander (who had 190 wins in seven years with the Phillies) to Chicago for three-game winner Mike Pendergast and catcher Pickles Dillhoefer and $55,000 in cash. At first, Baker pumped up the trade as a great thing for the Phillies, but he later admitted he made the trade because he needed the money.

Endurance

By Saam was the voice of Philadelphia baseball from 1938 to 1975. He called games for both the Phillies and the A's at a time when only home games were announced live. When the teams began taking announcers on the road in 1950, Saam went with the A's. He returned full time with the Phillies in 1955, when the A's moved to Kansas City. By the time he retired, Saam announced more losing games than any home-team announcer in history.

He Calls 'Em as He Sees 'Em

Saam was a Hall of Fame announcer, but he wasn't without his slip-ups. In a game against the St. Louis Cardinals, Saam announced that the Cardinal batter hit a ground ball to short stop. His boothmate, Richie Ashburn frantically signaled that it was not a ground ball, but a home run. Saam simply added, "And it's outta here." At a game inside the new Astrodome, Saam announced that it was a beautiful night for baseball. "The flags are limp. There is no breeze at all."

25

Philadelphia Far North

One of the greatest moments in Phillies history happened away from the ballpark. On July 30, 1995, third baseman Mike Schmidt and center fielder Richie Ashburn were inducted into the Hall of Fame. Schmidty was a first-ballot inductee. Whitey was elected by the Veteran's Committee, after a long, unjustified wait. Hotel rooms in a 200-mile radius around Cooperstown were booked months in advance, so fans arrived by the busload—over 200 busloads—on the morning of the ceremony. Cooperstown estimated that over 30,000 Phillies fans showed up. Touched by the turnout, Richie Ashburn tried to make all those fans feel at home. "I wish I could tell you we had Tastykakes and pretzels here," he said, "but you're on your own."

A Different Hall of Fame . . . Or Should We Say Phame

The Phillie Phanatic had his enshrinement into immortality on August 15, 2005, as a member of the inaugural class of the Mascot Hall of Fame. The Phanatic's classmates were the Phoenix Gorilla and the San Diego Chicken.

Blame It on Wilson

Woodrow Wilson was the first sitting president to attend a World Series game. He attended Game 2 of the 1915 World Series that pitted the Phillies against the Red Sox. Before Wilson's visit, the Phillies were 1-0. After his visit, the Phillies went 0-4.

Let's Play Two-and-a-Half

On July 17, 1918, Phillies rookie right-hander John "Mule" Watson gave up a single run in the 1st inning to the Cubs. In the 4th, the Phillies tied the game. The teams continued in a 1-1 battle until the 21st inning, when Watson gave up three consecutive singles to load the bases, then hit the next batter to force in the winning run. Watson's 21 innings is the longest outing ever by a Phillies pitcher.

Life Does Exist Outside of New York City

Because he wasn't a member of the New York trio of Mickey Mantle, Willie Mays, and Duke Snider, Richie Ashburn never got the credit he deserved as one of the game's best outfielders. Yet, Ashburn's lifetime batting average is higher than his New York contemporaries, and he holds the major league record of nine consecutive years with 400 put-outs.

Not Bad for Someone Not Named Bonds

In 2005, Bobby Abreu became only the third player to have at least seven consecutive seasons with 20 home runs and 20 stolen bases. Only Barry and Bobby Bonds have more.

1950 Was a Very Good Year . . . Or Not

1950 was supposed to be the Year of the Athletics. Connie Mack was celebrating his 50th year as manager of the team and the A's were picked to win the American League. Instead, the upstart Whiz Kids on the Phillies spoiled the party by winning the National League Pennant, while the A's began the slide that would soon lead to the team's departure from Philadelphia.

No Runs for You

Robin Roberts, Ken Johnson, Bubba Church, and Russ Meyer pitched
4 consecutive shut-out games in 1951.

Don't Throw So Hard

In a 1971 game, Phillies catchers Tim McCarver and Mike Ryan each broke his hand—in the same inning.

Mr. October, National League Version

Lenny Dykstra, the Phillies center fielder and lead-off hitter, had 4 home runs in the 1993 World Series, in addition to the 2 he hit in the NLCS. No other National League player has hit more home runs in a World Series; Barry Bonds tied the record in 2002.

One for the Ages

The 1993 World Series ripped the record books to shreds. The Phillies and the Blue Jays managed to break or tie 9 individual records, 19 team records, and 9 miscellaneous records, many of those thanks to the 4 hour, 14 minute Game 4 (longest game) and its 15-14 score (most total runs).

Gotta Take the Bad with the Good

Richie Allen won the 1964 Rookie of the Year with 29 home runs, 91 RBIs, 125 runs scored, a .318 batting average, 40 errors, and 138 strikeouts.

Why the Fans Shouldn't Vote

"It's amazing that fans want to see me play. It's kind of scary. I guess that's what's wrong with our society."—John Kruk after being elected by the fans as a starter in the 1993 All-Star Game.

The Downfall of Shoeless Joe Jackson

On August 31, 1919, the Phillies beat the Cubs, 3-0. Before the game, the Cubs president received telegrams warning him that the game was fixed for a Phillies win. William Veeck asked Chicago's baseball writers to conduct an investigation, which resulted in the Black Sox scandal.

You Stand There and I'll Jump in Your Arms

One of the greatest pictures in Phillies history—Mike Schmidt jumping on Tug McGraw after the final out in the 1980 World Series—was planned. Schmidt and McGraw plotted the leap on their drive to Veteran's Stadium before Game 6.

Once Is Not Enough

Richie Ashburn fouled off a pitch, which hit a female fan named Alice Roth and broke her nose. Ashburn fouled off another pitch, hitting Mrs. Roth again as she was being carried out of the stadium on a stretcher.

A Rose by Any Other Name

Why are they called the Phillies? Al Reach, who named the team, claimed "It tells you who we are and where we're from."

Four Times Is a Charm

Ed Delahanty, Chuck Klein, and Mike Schmidt have each hit 4 home runs in a game. All three are Hall of Famers. No other team has three players who have accomplished this feat.

Something About That Position

Dave Bancroft was the Phillies original spitfire shortstop. The sparkplug on the 1915 team that ended up in the World Series was also known for his outbursts and running at the mouth. Every time a pitcher made a good pitch, Bancroft would shout "Beauty!"

Voice of the Phillies

In 2002, Harry Kalas took his rightful place the Hall of Fame, receiving the Ford C. Frick Award for Broadcasting—an honor that every Phillies fan believes was not only well-deserved but should have come years ago. Harry the K was the second Phillies announcer to receive the Frick Award; By Saam being the first. Phillies beat writers Allen Lewis, Ray Kelly, and Bus Saidt were recipients of the J. Taylor Spink Award.

Even Harry Would Have Gone Hoarse in This Inning

In 1949, losing 3-2 to the Reds, the Phils exploded for 10 runs in the 8th inning, including five home runs. Andy Seminick had 2, and Schoolboy Rowe, Del Ennis, and Willie Jones each hit one.

What Is It with the Phillies and the Cubs?

The Phillies and Cubs seem to have quite an interesting history, but the game that stands out above all others came in May 1979. The final score, Phils 23, Cubs 22 was the highest scoring one-run game of the 20th century. Larry Bowa had 5 hits by the 6th inning. The Cubs Dave Kingman hit 3 homeruns. Mike Schmidt won it in the top of the 10th with his second homer of the day.

The Rodney Dangerfield Team

With the Baker Bowl crumbling around them, the Phillies moved to Shibe Park on July 1, 1938, sharing the stadium with the Athletics until the A's left town in 1955. Eventually, Shibe Park was renamed Connie Mack Stadium, and, until they moved into the Vet in 1971, the Phillies played their games in a stadium named for the manager of their former cross-town rivals.

Go the World Series, Get a Nickname

The 1950 team was called the Whiz Kids because of their youth and talent. The 1980 team was called the Cardiac Kids, largely due to all of those down-to-the-wire games in the NCLS. The 1983 team was called the Wheeze Kids, a collection of veteran ballplayers. The 1993 team were called the Broad Street Bellies, for reasons that probably do not need to be explained.

Cherry Hill Phils

When the city couldn't decide on a location for a new stadium in the late 1960s, Phillies owner Bob Carpenter bought 80 acres in Cherry Hill, NJ. Carpenter claimed he didn't buy the land for the new stadium, but the city soon decided on a site in South Philadelphia.

No Sitting on the Job

"The toughest thing about managing is standing up for nine innings."—Paul "Pope" Owens, long-time general manager who served two stints as the Phillies field manager.

Mickey Must Have Practiced

On September 20, 1992, Mickey Morandini became the first second baseman in baseball history to execute an unassisted triple play. He was the first only because his teammate Randy Ready didn't do it a year earlier. Ready caught a line drive, touched second base, and then threw the ball to first for the third out. When told he could have had an unassisted triple play if he would have simply tagged the runner off first, Ready said, "Well, I don't practice that."

Picking up Where He Left Off

On June 10, 1981, first baseman Pete Rose tied Stan Musial's National League hit record. Anticipation for breaking the record was put on hold for two months during a baseball strike. Rose was finally able to break the record on August 10, the day baseball returned.

Is It Over Yet?

The Phillies were scheduled to begin a doubleheader with the Padres at 4:35 pm on July 2, 1993. The first game was riddled with rain delays and didn't end until 1:00 am on July 3. The second game began at 1:26 am and ended up going extra innings. All told, the entire night of baseball took 12 hours, 5 minutes. Actual game time for the doubleheader was 5 hours, 36 minutes.

There Is No "I" in Team

"Different people, different backgrounds, different ideals . . . We walk in different doors at the beginning of the day, and we walk out of different doors at the end of the day. But when it is time to go out on that field, we all go through the same door."—Scott Rolen, Phillies third baseman, 1996–2002.

The Numbers Speak for Themselves

Steve Carlton's numbers at the end of the 1972 season: 27 wins. 10 losses. 1.98 ERA. 41 starts. 30 complete games. 341 innings pitched. 310 strikeouts.

Talented Players Need Not Apply

Phillies president William Baker was a well-known cheapskate. He would sell or trade his best players rather than pay them their worth.

The Baker Bowl's dimensions and its short right-field fence gave Chuck Klein Hall of Fame numbers. It looked like Klein could break Babe Ruth's homerun record. Baker installed a 20-foot-high screen over the right field fence, preventing Klein from hitting too many homers, which allowed Baker to avoid giving Klein a pay increase.

A Philly Original

Al Reach, the original owner of the Phillies, was the original professional baseball player. In 1865, Reach became the first man to sign a contract to be paid for playing ball. He played for the original version of the Philadelphia Athletics.

What Could Have Been

Hank Aaron was one of many African American players who tried out with the Phillies. But the Phillies, very slow to integrate, sent Aaron on his way, telling him the team would call if they were interested. They never called, and Aaron signed with the Braves.

It Did Happen Eventually

The first African American player on the Phillies was John Kennedy,
who joined the team in 1957. Kennedy's career
lasted 5 games and 2 at bats.

What Happened In-Between?

The Phillies won their first game and their last game
in the 20th century.

Did Congress Approve This Purchase?

In 1910, First Lady Nellie Taft purchased the Baker Bowl and leased it to the Phillies for 99 years.

Where Will They Put the Umpire?

"When Lefty and I die, they're going to bury us 60 feet 6 inches apart."—Tim McCarver, whose main role with the Phillies was to catch for Steve Carlton.

Quickie

Phillies pitcher Lee Meadows and Giants pitcher Jesse Barnes combined to pitch a game that lasted only 51 minutes. The final score of that September 28, 1919 game was 6-1 (Giants) with a combined 18 hits. Presumably, there was a lot of first ball swinging.

Equal Rights

In 1946, the Phillies hired the first female scout, Edith Houghton.

Sluggo Must Be a Phillies Fan

The tradition of kids watching games through the knotholes in fences began at the Baker Bowl. Kids would drill holes at the fence near the 15th Street gate, where they could see centerfield and the scoreboard. Eventually, these kids would be allowed into the game with a discounted ticket.

The 500 Homer Club

Mike Schmidt hit 548 home runs. Robin Roberts gave up 505 home runs.

When I Grow Up, I Want to Be . . .

Jim Bunning became a U.S. Senator from Kentucky. Gavvy Cravath was a justice of the peace in Long Beach, California. Lenny Dykstra owns a chain of carwashes. Jim Lonborg became a dentist.

The Real Rocky

Shortstop Larry Bowa was cut three times from his high school team, was ignored during the free agent draft, and should have been demoted to the minors halfway through his rookie year. Bowa ended up a 5-time All Star, had over 2100 hits, and was arguably the best defensive shortstop of the 70s.

We Don't Want Him, You Take Him

After the 1969, the Phillies worked out a trade with the St. Louis Cardinals, Curt Flood for Richie Allen, with a couple of other players tossed in. Flood made history by refusing the trade and precipitating free agency. The Phillies could have made the trade null and void, but they were so anxious to rid themselves of Allen that they took another player offered by the Cardinals, Willie Montanez.

A Man Ahead of His Times

Bill Veeck nearly integrated baseball in Philadelphia, four years before Jackie Robinson joined the Dodgers. The Phillies were in financial ruins. Veeck worked out a deal with Phils' owner Gerry Nugent to stock the team with players from the Negro League. Unfortunately, baseball commissioner Kenesaw Mountain Landis fought against integration and, with National League President Ford Frick, arranged for the league to buy the Phillies instead.

Nowhere to Go But Up

The Phillies finished their first season at 17-81.

September Swoon

The 1964 collapse will live in Philadelphia infamy. However, late-season meltdowns are a regular part to any Phillies season. The 2003 team could have won the wild card if it could have beaten Florida in the last weeks of the season. In 1976, the Phils were up 15½ games in late August and nearly lost the lead to Pittsburgh in September.

The Guy Deserved a Ring

Pete Rose has been given the credit of getting the Phillies over the final hump and into the World Series. But the guy who most likely had the most to do with putting the team into a position to compete was Dave Cash. Cash was only with the team for three seasons, but his leadership, his positive attitude, and his skill as a second baseman helped the young team around him mature. Cash left the team after the 1976 season as a free agent, but he left behind a team better prepared to make a championship run.

No Wasted Time

Darren Daulton led the league in RBIs in 1992 with 109, the first
player to do so with less than 500 at bats.

Walk Much?

Darren Daulton, John Kruk, and Lenny Dykstra each had over 100 walks in the 1993 season.

Who Names Their Kid Stumpy?

Everybody has a nickname in baseball. Names get shortened (like Schills, for Curt Schilling) or are given a "Y" ending (like Schmidty) or both (like Eisy for Jim Eisenreich). Today's team has Pat the Bat Burrell, J-Roll (Jimmy Rollins), and J-Mike (Jason Michaels). Over the years, players called Nails, Gnat, Bubba, Beauty, Squack, Wild Thing, Highpockets, Cupid, Pickles, Bull, Lefty, and Mighty Mouse took the field for the Fightin' Phils.

Perhaps You Knew My Dad

Terry Francona, the Phillies manager from 1997–2000, is the son of
former Phillies outfielder, Tito Francona.

Youth Will Be Served

The youngest Phillies player was Putsy Caballero who was 16 years old when he joined the ball club in 1944. The youngest Phillies player to appear in a World Series was 22-year-old Marty Bystrom, in 1980.

They'd Never Be Confused with Charlie Hustle

In a May 30, 1895 game, four Phillies batters were thrown out at first base by the right fielder.

Get the Ice Ready in the Clubhouse

Jack Scott was the last pitcher to pitch complete games on both ends of a doubleheader. The Phillies hurler beat the Reds in the first game, 3-1, and lost the second game 3-0, on June 19, 1927.

Don't I Know You from Somewhere?

The Phillies have had plenty of famous last names on the team over the years: Brett, DiMaggio, Maddux, Giambi, Coveleski, and Torre, to name a few. However, the first names were Ken, Vince, Mike, Jeremy, Harry, and Frank.

Everybody Knew His Name

Juan Samuel had 701 official at bats in 1984, the most
ever by a Phillies hitter.

The Game Is Secondary

Opening Day is always a big event for the Phillies. Over the years, they've had tight-rope walkers, the first ball brought in by a skydiver, and other stunts. But when the Phillies won their home opener in 2004, it was the first home Opening Day win since 1980.

Best Trades

Over the years, the Phillies built a reputation for bad trades or letting future super-stars land with other teams. But every so often the team made the right decision, even when it meant trading away a popular player. Arguably the best trade was Rick Wise for Steve Carlton. Wise was a good pitcher for the Cardinals, but Lefty became a Hall of Famer for the Phils. Other top-notch trades include Willie Montanez for Garry Maddox, Jason Grimsley for Curt Schilling, and Kevin Stocker for Bobby Abreu.

Like a Boomerang

A number of players left the Phillies, either by trade or free agency, but returned to the team a second time. Three players had three separate stints with the Phils: Bill Duggleby, Bill Hallman, and Chuck Klein.

Lifers (or So It Seemed)

No one played more games for the Phillies than Mike Schmidt. Most games at each position:

First Base: Fred Luderus, 1910–1920, 1,298 games
Second Base: Tony Taylor, 1960–71 and 1974–76, 1,003 games
Third Base: Mike Schmidt, 1972–1989, 2,212 games
Short Stop: Larry Bowa, 1970–1981, 1,667 games
Outfield: Richie Ashburn, 1948–1959, 1,785 games
Catcher: Red Dooin, 1902–1914, 1,124 games

Oh Yes, They Called Him the Streak

Jimmy Rollins had a 36-game hitting streak to end the 2005 season. Steve Carlton had 15 consecutive wins in 1972. John Coleman had 12 consecutive losses in 1883.

Imagine How an Outsider Would Be Treated

Del Ennis was born and raised in Philadelphia and played 10 seasons with his hometown Phillies. However, Ennis was booed by the home crowd nearly every time he came up to bat. It could be that the fans had higher expectations for the local boy who was one of the best hitters in Phillies history.

Player of the Week

Ever since the Player of the Week Award was instituted in 1973, two
Phillies players have won it five times: Mike Schmidt and Von Hayes

License, Registration, and Proof of Baseball Credentials, Please

"One time I got pulled over at four AM. I was fined seventy-five dollars for being intoxicated and four hundred for being with the Phillies."—Bob Uecker, who played for the Phillies in 1966–67.

Philley the Phillie

Dave Philley played only 3 years with his same-name team, but during his stay, he was one of the premier pinch hitters in the game. At the age of 38, Philley had 18 pinch hits for the Phils. In 1961, a year after he left Philadelphia, Philley set the all-time pinch-hit record in the American League, with the Red Sox.

Be Careful What You Wish For

On June 28, 2004, third baseman David Bell had hit a single, double, and home run. As Bell came up for his final at bat in the game, the announcers mused that it was unlikely that Bell would hit the triple. Due to his lack of speed, they agreed, Bell would need to get a funny bounce from the outfield wall and a lot of dumb luck. No sooner were the words spoken, Bell hit a long fly ball that bounced off the top of the fence and took a funny hop. Bell rolled into third for his cycle-completing triple, his first triple as a Phillie.

93

Pick the Winning Lottery Numbers Next

Veteran teammates decorated Scott Rolen's locker, announcing him the Rookie of the Year—before the season had begun. Rolen was a late-season call up in 1996, and just before his 130th at bat, which would have made him ineligible for rookie considerations the following year, Rolen's arm was broken by a pitch. Rolen was a unanimous choice for the award in 1997.

Thanks for Nothing

Curt Schilling won the National League Championship Series MVP in 1993, despite two no-decisions. He struck out 19 batters in 16 innings, including the first five batters he faced in the series opener.

The Importance of the Buddy System

"Don't leave all at once. Leave in groups of twos and threes. They are selling rocks out there, a dollar a pail, and this way they can't get us all at once."—Frank Sullivan, Phillies pitcher, when the Phillies returned from a road trip in which the final game ended the teams 23-game losing streak.

Lefties Rule!

The dimensions of the Baker Bowl were 272 to right, 408 in dead center, and 400 in left. It was a left-handed hitter's dream ballpark, and a right-handed pitcher's nightmare. It also helped to make Chuck Klein a Hall of Fame hitter.

Long Before Steroids

In 1894, the Phillies team batting average was .349. The average in the
National League was .309.

Unser, Grab Your Bat

In 1979, Del Unser set a Major League record by hitting pinch-hit home runs in three consecutive official at bats. In the midst of that streak, Unser walked, but because a bases on balls is not an official at bat, it kept his streak intact.

Charmed, Yet Clumsy

Lonnie Smith was a rookie in 1980, but he played an important role on the team, platooning with Greg Luzinski in left field and adding some excitement on the base paths with both his speed and his tendency to trip and fall as he ran. Smith lasted only two full seasons in Philadelphia, but he went on to win World Series rings with St. Louis and Kansas City, as well as pennants with the Atlanta Braves.

Sometimes You Win a Few

The Phillies have had 50 managers between 1883 and 2005. Of those
who have managed more than one season, twelve have a
career record above .500.